RAILWAY

• HALSGROVE •

SERIES

LAST DAYS OF STEAM
NORTHERN & EASTERN

Tony Butcher

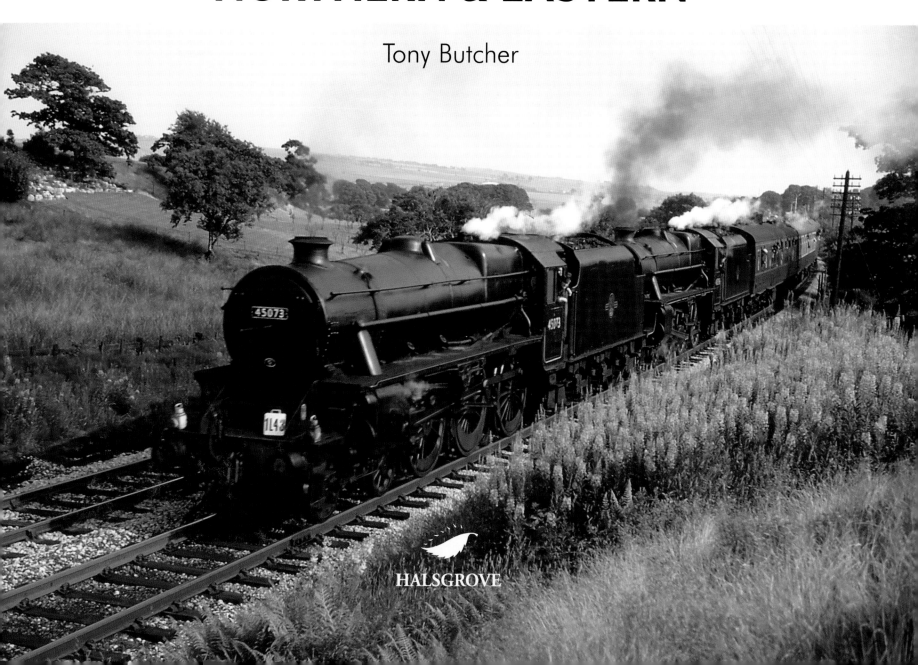

HALSGROVE

DEDICATION

For my wife Anne, whose excellent typing from my unreadable scribble has been essential to this and previous ventures, as well as her understanding and support over the years to my lifetime obsession, although tried to the limit many times.

And for my railway enthusiast son, David.

First published in Great Britain in 2015

British Library Cataloguing-in-Publication Data
A CIP record for this title is available from the British Library

ISBN 978 0 85704 273 6

HALSGROVE
Halsgrove House,
Ryelands Industrial Park,
Bagley Road, Wellington, Somerset TA21 9PZ
Tel: 01823 653777   Fax: 01823 216796
email: sales@halsgrove.com

Part of the Halsgrove group of companies.
Information on all Halsgrove titles is available at: www.halsgrove.com

Printed and bound in China by Everbest Printing Co Ltd

Title page image: With only seven days scheduled of BR steam left, Black 5s Nos.45073 and 45156 make light work of the climb up to Sough Tunnel near Entwistle with the willow herb in full flower hauling the MRTS/SVRS "Steam Farewell" tour of 28 July 1968 en route to Blackburn and Rose Grove from Skipton. From Rose Grove the last 8F No.48773 would take over for the last leg via Copy Pit to Manchester Victoria and Stockport.

INTRODUCTION

Like many my first interest in railways was focused on model railways and obtaining my first Hornby Dublo Set. In the early years after the war such things were in very short supply. My father managed to get a "Sir Nigel Gresley" set, which he said was about the only one left in London. This was followed by purchasing "Duchess of Atholl", so they were at least appropriate engines for this book. Some years later, however, a cousin of thirteen came to stay with us for a week. To keep my young visitor occupied during the week I took him up to Clapham Junction to do some train-spotting, and my interest in the real thing was reawakened.

In 1955 I was bought a very basic bellows camera for my birthday, which only had a 1/75 sec shutter which was hardly enough for even the slowest moving train. A few still shots were taken here and there but most of them very poor. The next year I graduated to a cheap but somewhat better 2¼ x 3¼ Kodak camera which at least had a 1/200 shutter speed and I started to take some reasonably good pictures, mainly where I lived down south.

In this period a visit was made to Edinburgh with my parents who were going to the Edinburgh Festival and I started to see some interesting LNER engines around Edinburgh Waverley and through Princes Street Gardens, as well as at Haymarket Shed. I was very taken by the old 4-4-0 engines of the D30 "Scot" and D34 "Glen" Classes and also the Scottish D11 "Directors". What fascinated me were all the weird and wonderful names: who's ever heard of an engine called "Luckie Mucklebackit!" I realised later that these names came from Sir Walter Scott's novels. Both the LNER and the LMS had inherited several classes of older good looking 4-4-0s. I could also mention the Midland Compounds and 2Ps, as well as the last of all the Great North of Scotland D40 4-4-0s of which only "Gordon Highlander" survived.

By this time I was about to go up to University in Birmingham and then became acquainted with the dark semi-underground depths of Birmingham New Street Station, but also the famous Lickey Incline. I travelled back and forth to my home by steam in this period and liked to catch the "Midlander" from Birmingham New Street.

During this period I took black and white shots of everyday steam where I could, within the limits of not having my own transport and studying at university. By this time I had graduated to an Agfa Isolette 2 square camera with a 1/500 sec shutter.

Although I was first and foremost a "Southern" man I did manage to make some sorties out to the King's Cross and Euston main lines in the University holidays, and saw many Pacifics out of London of both regions in action.

From the end of 1958 my time was taken up with getting married, finding a house and starting my first job, which rather put an end to my railway activities for three years. However, one bonus of these events was that all my wife's family came from Sunderland and several visits were made during the year to her aunt still living there. Then with Sunderland South Dock Shed only down the road and having a car by 1960, I saw a different world of numerous J27s, Q6s and K1s 0-6-0s in use with many collieries and therefore coal trains around. The highlight of these NE visits, however, was the Consett ore line where the mighty 9F 2-10-0s toiled up almost 10 miles of heavy gradients with 2 miles at 1 in 40 – 50 up to the summit at Anfield Plain with a 9F at each end hauling 600 tons of iron ore from Tyne Dock to the steelworks perched on a hill on the edge of Weardale. I did manage to start photographing steam engines again from mid 1961 when I then obtained my first 35mm camera fitted with a good 50mm lens and a range finder focusing. I continued to take only black and white until 1962, when I started to take some colour pictures in 2¼in square format, both colour negatives and transparencies. However, these were taken with a very basic Kodak camera belonging to my wife. It was not until mid-1963 that I started taking some 35mm colour transparencies. I still continued to take mainly black and white photographs throughout the BR years and only regularly took 35mm colour transparencies in the last years of British Steam from 1965 to '68.

GNSR D40 (BR No. 62277) "Gordon Highlander" waits to come off shed in the evening sun to doublehead the last leg of the 1963 "Scottish Rambler" back to Glasgow from Stranraer over the Ayrshire Moors.

This situation awakened my photographic interest in railway enthusiast specials, for which the locomotives were normally very well turned out if not immaculate, and were often the last survivors of classes that could by then be seen only with difficulty if at all in normal service. My holiday leave in those days was severely limited to three weeks and had to include my wife's holiday; that almost all these specials ran at weekends was therefore a big plus. A good steam tour had many attractions, all concentrated into the few hours available. The routes chosen, often circular in nature, were usually of particular interest, traversing little used cross country lines, freight-only branches and many other delightful branches often about to be closed of the pre-Beeching type.

Of particular interest in this period were the "Scottish Rambler" specials run once a year from 1962 to 1966, which used an array of Scottish steam and in particular used three or more of the four preserved engines restored to working order under the benevolent auspices of the Scottish Region General Manager. Namely the "Caledonian Single", the "Jones Goods", the last "Glen", and the GNSR 4-4-0 "Gordon Highlander" (but not used in 1966).

All my photography and chasing round the country was done driving an Austin A35 from 1960 to 1963 and then a basic 850cc Morris Mini from the end of 1963 to almost the end of steam in January 1968. It amazes me how well the little beast coped with all this, like toiling up to Carter Bar in the pouring rain en route to Scotland, when I had to cover the inside of the radiator grill with silver paper to avoid the distributor getting wet and shorting out!

Often, of course, the weather was not good, and efforts to capture the shots on 50 ASA Agfa colour transparency film were not always very successful. Partly because of this I continued taking a lot of black and white shots up to the end of BR steam, initially on 35mm FP3 film and latterly on 2¼ inch FP3 and 400 ASA TRIX, the latter much the more useful in dull weather. 35mm 25 ASA Kodachrome, although the best film, was usually used only in sunny weather because of its low speed. In fact looking back at my black and white work, I am surprised on occasions to see how well a shot has come out, even though the weather was very poor, which would have been hopeless for colour in those non-digital days.

However, I have always liked black and white photography. I have done all my own developing and printing over the years. Perhaps also black and white photographs of the BR steam age give a more nostalgic and historic impression than colour of the "Great Days of Steam". As this is largely a black and white book of photographs I hope they convey some of this feeling.

Tony Butcher
Crawley Down, 2015

LNER MAIN LINE
KING'S CROSS AND LONDON AREA

Having obtained my first cameras with a 1/250 second and then a 1/500 second shutter speed in the first two years of my photography in 1956 and 1957, I ventured out to the main lines out of London. Apart from the Southern Region main line out of Waterloo near my home, I made several day outings to the King's Cross LNER main line between Wood Green and Hadley Wood in this period.

I was greeted with a constant parade of all classes of Pacific with the occasional V2 2-6-2. I hardly took any photographs of the B1s and B17s on the Cambridge Buffet Expresses, let alone the odd freight. I travelled out from King's Cross on the locals headed by the numerous N2 0-6-2 tanks in the old suburban coaches, but never took a single picture of one. The northbound trains from King's Cross face an 8 mile continuous climb at 1 in 200 between Wood Green and Potters Bar, which meant they were always working quite hard. All images were taken on 5 April 1957 unless otherwise stated.

The first of the V2 Class 2-6-2s No.60800 "Green Arrow" speeds into New Barnet Station with an up express. (13.6.57)

An immaculate A4 Pacific No.60007 "Sir Nigel Gresley" storms up to Hadley Wood with the morning "Talisman" Express limited to eight coaches for the fast run to Edinburgh.

Gleaming A3 Pacific in original condition No.60108 "Gay Crusader" powers up the
bank out of New Barnet about two thirds of the way up the climb with a down express.

Opposite: A4 No.60032 "Gannet" steams up from
New Barnet in fine style with a down express.

A4 Pacific No.60006 "Sir Ralph Wedgwood" speeds down from Hadley Wood
Tunnel on 5 April 1957. Note the tunnel bottleneck being rebuilt to take four tracks
in the distance. The slow line here only went into a holding loop.

Opposite: In the same direction A4 No.60015 "Quicksilver" bursts under the bridge
at Wood Green Station with only a few miles to go to King's Cross.

The unique W1 4-6-4 No.60700 climbs up to Hadley Wood with a semi-fast express. The W1 was a common sight from King's Cross being shedded there, having been rebuilt from the high pressure water tube boiler experimental locomotive. Based on its tractive effort this was the most powerful locomotive in Britain at the time.

The very different appearance from the A1 Pacifics and other A2s is apparent as A2/2 Pacific No 60502 "Earl Marischal" powers up the grade from New Barnett. The locomotive was one of six engines rebuilt by Thompson in 1943 from Gresley's P2 Class 2-8-2 "Cock of the North" Mikados introduced in 1934. The A2/2s were not noted for their fleetness of foot and they hungered for coal to the extent of being known as the 'miners' friends'.

Gresley B17/4 Class 4-6-0 No.61652 "Darlington" speeds into Wood Green Station with a northbound Cambridge Express. This big class of 73 of these quite modern looking engines was introduced in 1928, with rebuilding going on into the 1940s, but they had a reputation for rough riding, and all were withdrawn by 1960 and most by 1955. (7.8.56)

EDINBURGH AND HAYMARKET SHED

Class D11 "Scottish Director" 4-4-0 No.62694 "James Fitzjames" outside Edinburgh Haymarket Shed in company with a Caledonian 0-6-0. 24 D11s were modified to comply with the lower North British loading gauge. The Scottish Directors outlived their English counterparts by two years, but most had been withdrawn by the end of 1960/61, although one or two survived until 1963. (30.8.56)

Already an 'Old Stager' D11 4-4-0 No.62678 "Luckie Mucklebackit" stands in steam at Haymarket Shed. Note the buckled front plate. (30.8.56)

A2/1 Pacific No.60510 "Robert the Bruce" stands outside Edinburgh Haymarket Shed with a rather austere double stovepipe chimney as used on several of the class. (30.8.56)

Peppercorn A2 Pacific No.60528 "Tudor Minstrel" with a more attractive single lipped chimney stands outside Haymarket Shed and is getting some attention from the crew before heading north. Shedded at Dundee at this time it was still shedded there when one of the last three operational A2s together with 60530 and 60532 at the end of Scottish steam in August 1966. (30.8.56)

A1 No.60159 "Bonnie Dundee" steams out of Edinburgh Waverley through Princes Street Gardens with a Perth – Aberdeen Express. (31.8.56)

B1 No.61261 accelerates out of Edinburgh Waverley through Princes Street Gardens with a semi-fast to the north. (31.8.56)

North British "Scott" Class D30 4-4-0 No.62626 "Cuddie Headrigg" starts a Perth train out of the gloom of Edinburgh Princes Street Station, built originally to serve as the Caledonian Railway Terminus. The D30 and D11 Class names were a joy to behold for a Southern man venturing north of the border, the names coming from Sir Walter Scott's novels. All of this Class had been withdrawn by 1960 and 62626 was one of the last ones to survive. The very similar "Glens" had slightly smaller driving wheels for the West Highland Line gradients at 6ft 0 ins compared with 6ft 6 ins. (31.3.56)

Immaculate North British Class J83 0-6-0 tank No.68481 stands in Edinburgh Waverly Station while acting as No.1 "Station Pilot". (31.8.56)

1963 SCOTTISH RAMBLER

The "Scottish Rambler" Rail Tours ran from 1962 to 1966. Usually a four day event in April, each tour employed a variety of engine classes using interesting and often freight only lines around Scotland, but in particular the use of three or all four (not in 1966) of the Scottish preserved engines put back into working order by the benevolent Scottish Region manager. These events were a joy to behold and will be long remembered by those who were lucky enough to see any of them.

Preserved Caledonian Single No.123 halts at Killin Junction with the snow still falling on (12.4.63) with the first day of the 1963 "Scottish Rambler", having just fought its way up the 5 miles at 1 in 60 of Glen Ogle in a snowstorm. It only just managed not to slip to a stand on its single driver up to the summit of 914 ft at Glenoglehead, while en route to Crianlarich from Callander.

Class J37 0-6-0 No.64718 fly shunts its passenger stock over the viaduct outside the now freight-only branch terminus of Leslie (Fife), due to no run round facility being available in the station, on the occasion of the second day of the "Scottish Rambler". (13.4.63)

The preserved North British "Glen" 4-4-0 No.256 "Glen Douglas" prepares to leave Rumbling Bridge after a photo stop, while traversing the Devon Valley line from Kinross to Alloa on the second day of the joint SLS/BLS "Scottish Rambler" 13 April 1963. At Alloa a J36 took over for the run up the branch to Alva.

Ex North British J36 class 0-6-0, No.65323 having run round its train pauses in the evening sun at Alva – by then a freight-only terminus close to the Ochil Hills. The locomotive then returned up the short branch to Alloa with the Easter 1963 "Scottish Rambler" tour on 13 April, where the "Glen" took over once more for the return to Edinburgh Waverley.

Further down the line to St Boswells the B1 pulls forward off the train at the small junction of Roxburgh in preparation for heading the SLS special tender-first down the freight only branch to Jedburgh, seen diverging to the right. The B1 from St Margaret's Shed has hauled the train from Edinburgh via Tweedmouth and Coldstream to St Boswells.

On the third day of the "Scottish Rambler" B1 Class No.61324 comes off its train at Coldstream in order to allow an LMS 2-6-0 (just seen at rear of train) to head the train down the freight only branch to Wooler, by this time the terminus of the line which once ran through to Alnwick. Later the B1 continued to St Boswells and up the other section of the truncated branch to Greenlaw and back, and thence to Hawick on the Waverley route where the train was taken over by A3 Pacific No. 60051 "Blink Bonny" in the pouring rain to complete its journey to Carlisle. (14.4.63).

Making heavy smoke "Jubilee" Class No.45588 "Kashmir" pauses at the isolated Loch Skerrow platform for water in the course of traversing the former Portpatrick and Wigtownshire Joint Line to Stranraer from Carlisle with the fourth and final day of the SLS/BLS "Scottish Rambler", but would stop at Newton Stewart to allow a Caledonian 2F to take the train down the branch to Whithorn. The passing platform was located several miles from the nearest road amid the remote moors of Kirkcudbrightshire. (15.4.63)

The Caledonian 2F "Jumbo" No.57375 runs through a gated crossing on the way down the line to Whithorn. The gates had to be operated manually by the guard on this trip over the branch.

The ex Caledonian 2F 0-6-0 No.57375 arrives at the branch terminus station of Whithorn having travelled the freight-only branch from Newton Stewart. Designated the Caledonian "Standard Goods" these engines introduced between 1883 and 1887 became by far the biggest class on the CR.244 were built and all were gone by the end of 1963, this engine being one of the last survivors.

The preserved "Caledonian Single" No.123 halts at Luib on the Caledonian line to Oban having fought its way up the 5 miles1-60 off Glen Ogle on its single driver in a snowstorm, only just managing not to slip to a stand. The train proceeded to Crianlarich Upper via the loop onto the West Highland line where it turned on the turntable, and then returned to Glasgow with the first day of the "Scottish Rambler" on 12 April 1963.

Preserved ex North British D34 Class 4-4-0, No.256 "Glen Douglas" pauses at Dunfermline
Upper Station for water while heading the second day of the 1963 "Scottish Rambler" from
Edinburgh to Ladybank and the Devon Valley line via Kinross to Alloa, on 13 April 1963.

A rather dirty J37 Class 0-6-0, No.64603 is ready to leave South Queensferry Goods for the junction with the main line at Dalmeny. "Glen Douglas" is at the other end of the train having headed down the branch from Edinburgh Waverley. This J37 only assisted the "Glen" up and down the branch from Dalmeny Junction.

The "Glen" then continued to Thornton Junction where another J37 No.64618, seen here in immaculate condition, took over for a visit to the Leslie Branch from the junction at Markinch. The passenger stock had to be fly shunted back over the viaduct immediately outside the station in order for the J37 to run round. The branch served the paper mill at Leslie, but had been closed to passengers for many years.

The J37 is seen here in the station at Leslie before running round.

One of the four preserved pre-Grouping locomotives returned to traffic by the Scottish Region in the early 1960s, North British "Glen" 4-4-0 No.256 "Glen Douglas" runs into the station of Strathmiglo on the line from Ladybank to Kinross before continuing to Alloa via the Devon Valley line with the 1963 "Scottish Rambler" on 13 April 1963. One of 32 locomotives built to a design of Reid between 1913 and 1920 the "Glens" were traditionally associated with the West Highland line.

Ex LNER B1 Class No.61324 having run round the loop pauses at Duns in typically Border country scenery after heading the SLS/BLS Easter "Scottish Rambler" tender-first, up the branch from Reston on the main Berwick – Edinburgh main line on 14 April 1963. This branch was previously a through line connecting with the "Waverley" route at St Boswells, but was cut in the floods of 1948 and was thereafter worked only for freight as separate branches from each end.

"Jubilee" Class No.45588 "Kashmir" prepares to depart from the closed rural station of Shieldhill while traversing the former Caledonian Branch from Locherbie to Dumfries having started the day at Carlisle on the final day of the SLS/BLS "Scottish Rambler" on 15 April 1963. The "Jubilee" then headed the train to Stranraer after pausing for trips down two branch lines en route with other engines.

Ex Caledonian Drummond 2F 0-6-0 No.57375, built in 1884 from an 1883 design, makes heavy smoke after arrival at the overgrown terminus of Garlieston, on the short branch from the junction at Millisle which once saw specials to the Isle of Man. Because the branch was by then freight only with weight restrictions, the passengers of the SLS/BLS "Scottish Rambler" were conveyed in open wagons from Millisle. The 0-6-0 had earlier headed the special down the length of the Whithorn peninsula on the former Portpatrick & Wigtownshire joint line from Newton Stewart to Whithorn.

The preserved HR "Jones'Goods" 4-6-0 No.103 and GNSR 4-4-0 "Gordon Highlander" No.49 (ex BR No.62277) prepare to come off shed at Stranraer to head the 1963 "Scottish Rambler" back over the moors to Glasgow via Barhill and Ayr to Glasgow on 15 April 1963. "Gordon Highlander" was the last of the Class (designated D40 by the LNER and British Railways) operational and was withdrawn in 1956, but restored to working order in the early 1960s, before being placed in the Glasgow Museum of Transport after 1965.

Preserved HR "Jones Goods" 4-6-0 No.103 and GNSR 4-4-0 "Gordon Highlander" pause at Barr Hill in the fading light for water while double heading the final stage of the 1963 "Scottish Rambler" from Stranraer back to Glasgow via Girvan up the steep gradients over the Aryshire Moors on 15 April 1963.

LMS MAIN LINE AND CAMDEN SHED

Beside the LNER main line, I also made several visits to the LMS main line out of Euston, where expresses were almost exclusively in the hands of the Duchesses, Princess Royals, and Royal Scots, and like the main lines of the other regions there were a number of named trains running, which added to the spectacle. Again having no transport of my own at this time I travelled out on the local trains usually headed by the BR Class 4 2-6-4 Standard tanks to Watford and the Bushey and Oxley area. I also photographed out on Camden Bank and visited Camden Shed, but unfortunately my 2¼" square camera sprung a fault that day letting light through a pinhole in the bellows. This caused me to lose a number of useful photographs.

Adorned with the handsome "Caledonian" headboard, "Duchess" Class Pacific No.46239 "City of Chester" powers up Camden bank in effortless Stanier Pacific style, surefooted and with steam to spare. This express was the successor to the pre-war "Coronation Scot", between Euston and Glasgow Central and ran with a relatively light load of eight to nine carriages. (30.7.57)

Rebuilt "Royal Scot" Class 4-6-0 No.46119 "Lancashire Fusilier" speeds through Bushey and Oxhey on an up express, with only 16 miles more to go to Euston. No.46119, allocated to Crewe North, was rebuilt in 1944 and withdrawn in 1963. In August 1950 she was involved in a collision at Penmaenmawr when heading the up "Irish Mail". At 3.a.m., with sixteen on, and doing almost 70m.p.h., she collided with a 2-6-0 running light, six persons being killed and many injured. Although seriously damaged, No.46119 was rebuilt and put back in service in 1951. (3.4.57)

"The Ulster Express" constituted the principal LMS service to Northern Ireland, running between Euston and Heysham, connecting with steamers plying to Belfast. Inaugurated in 1927, it was invariably a "Royal Scot" or later a Pacific turn. Here "Duchess" No.46244 "King Gerorge VI", of Camden Shed, rests by the buffer stops at Euston after bringing the express in on 30 July 1957.

"Jubilee" Class No.45737 "Atlas" speeds past the side of Watford Shed with an up express from Birmingham. (3.4.57)

"Princess Royal" No.46207 "Princess Arthur of Connaught" enters Euston with the "Shamrock Express" from Holyhead. Note the little boys trainspotting at the extreme end of the platform. No health and safety restrictions then! (3.4.57)

"Princess Royal" No.46203 "Princess Margaret Rose" peers out of Camden Shed while on the left
"Jubilee" No.45601 "British Guiana" can just be identified from its number in the gloom. (3.4.57)

Appropriately named "Duchess" No.46247 – "City of Liverpool" having come off the "Ulster Express" stands at the side of Camden Shed on a misty morning with the coaling tower looming in the background. (3.4.57)

"Princess Royal" Class 4-6-2 No.46203 "Princess Margaret Rose" backs out of Euston to Camden Shed having brought in an up express on 3 April 1957. These first Stanier Pacifics had a long, lean look compared to the later "Duchesses" – partly due to them not being fitted with smoke deflectors. The smaller diameter boiler of this earlier class did not necessitate these.

Midland 2F No.58148 looks very dirty, but is bathed in sunshine, as it trundles along the Leicester West Bridge Branch in a country setting with a rake of wagons bound for the factory on 22 November 1963.

Opposite: One of the last three Midland 2Fs No.58148 kept for working the freight-only Leicester West Bridge Branch shunts at Glenfield Station. The 2Fs were kept in service due to the tight clearances through Glenfield Tunnel at the east end of the station prohibiting the use of larger engines. A week or so later their use had ceased at the factory at Desford. (22.11.63)

The 2F arrives at the factory at Desford with is load, after I had enjoyed a short footplate ride. The 15E shed code denotes the three engines are shedded at Coalville. What a pity the use of these quaint old engines of 1875 original vintage (rebuilt with Belpaire firebox in 1917) was then about to cease.

NORTH EAST STEAM – SUNDERLAND AND BLYTH

I was introduced to North Eastern steam after meeting my wife, as her parents came from Sunderland, and thereafter quite frequent visits were made to her relatives in that area. This opened my eyes to the parade of freight workings, particularly out of Sunderland South Dock Shed and down the coast to the Ryhope area feeding the numerous collieries, as well as power stations. Large numbers of J27 0-6-0s, and Q6 0-8-0s both of relatively old ex NE design vintage (1906 and 1913 respectively) were still hard at work as were a small number of the larger Q7 0-8-0s. More modern engines such as B1 and K1 Classes were also common. The large A8 Pacific tanks had unfortunately not long been withdrawn from local service to Durham and elsewhere by the time I visited the area.

Class Q7 No.63469 0-8-0 of North East Raven design is prepared for the next duty outside Sunderland (South Dock) on 5 August 1959, with air pumps previously used on the Consett ore trains still in evidence.

J27 0-6-0 No.65788 blasts up the climb from Sunderland South Dock at Ryhope with colliery empties probably for Silksworth Colliery. (11.3.65)

K1 No.62030 works hard up-grade along the coast line near Ryhope en route from Sunderland to Teesside with the remnants of a not-unusual sea mist around as seen by any distant views. (11.3.65)

Still clean from a recent works visit at this late date, J27 65789 pounds past Winning Junction with a coal train from North Blyth to the collieries. My Mini is on the left with which I covered all my steam journeys from late 1963 until the end of 1967. (13.3.65)

Two of the remaining four J27s present at the much smaller North Blyth Shed are seen inside the shed, namely Nos.65789 and 65812 on 18 May 1967, by now getting late in the day for North East steam.

Q6 no. 63445 takes water outside the roundhouse at Sunderland Shed, while on the left a J27 stands outside the 'straight' shed on a misty March morning. (11.3.65)

A line of five withdrawn A8 Class 4-6-2Ts at Sunderland Shed, (Nos. 69889, 69858, 69856, 69873 and 69883) on 5 August 1959. Their duties in this area to Durham and beyond had unfortunately recently been curtailed. All were withdrawn by the end of 1960.

J27 No.65817 waits at Ryhope Junction up the line from Sunderland South Dock
Shed to run round before making for one of the collieries with empty trucks. (7.8.64)

A relatively clean J27 0-6-0 No.65834 climbs up from North Blyth with an empty coal train for the collieries. (13.3.65)

Q6 No.63459 sticks its head out of the back of West Hartlepool's roundhouse in the last days of North Eastern steam.

Work stained K1 No.62022 waits its next turn of duty at North Blyth Shed while a Coal Board Peckett tank runs down to the staithes with a loaded coal train. (13.3.65)

Q6 No.63354 works hard to pull a long train of coal wagons tender first past Winning Junction box, again with my Mini in the distance.

N7/4 Class 0-6-2T No.69621 waits at Liverpool Street to head to Palace Gate and Chingford on the first leg of the original LCGB "Great Eastern Suburban" rail tour on 7 April 1962, where a J15 took over for the rest of the tour. The special was repeated on 28 April 1962, and proved to be the last steam special on the London Great Eastern section. Note the diesels, already in dominance. No.69621 was the last survivor of the original engines built by the Great Eastern Railway, and only 13 of the class remained in service by this date.

Close-up of GE J15 No.65476 running round at Ongar in the sun on 28 April 1962.

One of the last active ex-GER J15 Class 0-6-0s, of 1883 vintage, No.65476 pounds tender-first up the steep gradient out of Ongar returning up the branch to Epping – on the return run to Stratford with the LCGB "Great Eastern Suburban" rail tour on 28 April 1962. This was a repeat run and the last steam hauled special over the former Great Eastern lines from Liverpool Street. Of this originally very large class only 13 were not withdrawn by this time.

The already preserved by then B12/3 ex LNER Class 4-6-0 No.61572 with the M&GNJRS "Wandering 1500" rail tour joins the main freight-only Stratford-on-Avon & Midland Junction line at Towcester on the spur from Blisworth, having travelled up the Midland main line from Broad Street via Bedford and Olney to Northampton Castle, where the engine took water on shed before taking the spur at Blisworth.

The ex LNER B12/3 No.61572 makes heavy smoke about to leave the long closed station of Byfield on the former Stratford-on-Avon & Midland Junction line, en route from Blisworth to Stratford-on-Avon on 5 October 1963 with the Midland & Great Northern Joint Railway Preservation Society "Wandering 1500" rail tour, unfortunately in very poor weather. Subsequently it returned to London Broad Street via Leamington and the LMS main line. This was its only special run before a long period of storage (originally saved by the Norwich Shed Master) and then restoration. The engine finally emerged in working order resplendent in apple green and then BR lined black livery on the North Norfolk Railway after many years and is the only operational inside cylinder 4-6-0 left in Britain.

LMS SPECIALS

Super G2A 0-8-0 No.48930 of original 1912 vintage (but rebuilt in 1936) speeds through the long-closed station at Stanbridgeford en route from Luton (Bute Street) to Banbury Merton Street (LNWR) via Bletchley and Verny Junction with the "Banburian" tour of the South Bedfordshire Locomotive Club on the 22 September 1962. Having been rebuilt in 1936 these engines always looked a lot older than they were, particularly as they retained the cast iron smoke box door which stopped a number plate being fixed on the front.

One of the last surviving Midland 2P 4-4-0s No.40646 in beautiful external condition pilots a Fowler 2-6-2 condensing tank No.40026 (originally intended for working to Moorgate) into Bedford Midland Station with the SLS "Seven Branches Line" rail tour of 14 April 1962. The 2P had hauled the train from Birmingham to Northampton and then over the Midland branch via Olney to Bedford double-heading with the 3MT. No.40026 then took over to Hitchin, where the preserved Great Northern J52 0-6-0 tank (now in green livery as No. 1247) waited to take the train to Luton (Bute Street) via Hertford North, where the 2P was waiting to take over once more for the return journey back to Birmingham.

The Super G2A No.48930 pulls out of Buckingham Station with the SBLC "Banburian". Beyond this point to Banbury the line was already closed to all but freight, and the County Town had by now only a diesel rail car service. The station was noted for its display of gardens and general upkeep, and had won many awards.

The Midland 2P 4-4-0 No.40646 shedded at Bescot (where only three of the class were left in service), looking immaculate, speeds out of Linslade Tunnels in the last of the evening light with the SLS "Seven Branch Lines" rail tour returning to Birmingham via Leighton Buzzard and the LMS main line. What a pity this engine had not been taken into preservation directly.

The last known special to use a Midland 3F 0-6-0 was with No.43658 seen here approaching Castle Donnington en route from Burton-on-Trent to Derby (Midland) via Trent with the third leg of the LCGB "Midland Ltd" on 14 October 1962, having taken over from a J11 0-6-0 which had come on at Nottingham Victoria. Dating from 1885 there were only 20 left working by this date. This tour started from Marylebone and took the Great Central route to Nottingham Victoria hauled by B16 4-6-0 No.61418. It was also notable as one of the last rail tours to use a "un-rebuilt Patriot" in this case 4-6-0 No.45543 "Home Guard" from Derby to London St Pancras.

"Royal Scot" Class 4-6-0 No.46155 "The Lancer" approaches Peterborough East having just come off the ex-MR line from Luffenham at Felton Road Junction in charge of "The Pennine Limited" rail tour from St Pancras via Market Harborough organized by the LCGB on 19 September 1964. A1 Pacific No.60128 "Bongrace" of Peterborough Shed took over at this point to Sheffield Victoria and Retford. The section of line from this direction now forms the site of the Nene Valley Railway between Wansford and Orton Mere. Out of a total of 71 engines some 57 had already been condemned and the days of the "Royal Scots" were distinctly numbered, the last one being the later preserved No.46115 "Scots Guardsman", surviving until January 1965 for a last special.

Black 5 No.44680 attacks the 4 miles up Gresford Bank at 1in 82 on its way from Birkenhead and Chester to Birmingham returning with the second of the SLS specials on 5 March 1967, run to mark the end of the Birkenhead – Paddington service.

A smart smartly turned out 4F 0-6-0 No.44414 pauses for photographs at Bradwell Station returning up the by now freight-only branch from Newport Pagnell to Wolverton, having run from Luton (Bute Street) via Dunstable and Leighton Buzzard on the main line to gain the branch with the South Bedfordshire Locomotive Club's "Cobbler" rail tour on 19 September 1964. The branch had been closed to passengers as recently as 7 September 1964, and was steam operated to the last. The special then headed to Wellingborough via Blisworth and Northampton (Bridge Street), where a second 4F took over for a run up the short Higham Ferrers Branch before returning to Luton Midland via Bedford.

Opposite: Well groomed "Jubilee" Class No.45721 "Impregnable" waits to depart from St Pancras Station with the LCGB "North Countryman" tour which it headed as far as Whitehall Junction, Leeds where V2, 2-6-2 No.60823 took over for the run to Carlisle on 6 June 1964. With no photo stops and passengers not allowed to get off the train at Leeds or Carlisle with engines changed at Whitehall Junction and outside Upperby Shed, photographic opportunities were very limited, quite apart from the very poor weather on this summer's day.

One of the last operational 4F 0-6-0s was brought all the way from Workington to haul the RCTS "The Midland Locomotives Requiem" of 16 October 1965. Immaculately turned out No.43953 is seen here leaving Nuneaton Abbey Street (Midland) Station (where the tour started) heading for Mansfield Town via Trent and Nottingham including a run up the freight-only branch to Glapwell Colliery. The 4F then returned to Nuneaton via Kirkby-in-Ashfield and the Great Central main line to Wigston. Somewhat surprisingly by this time as a last survivor, this engine was one of the older original Fowler Midland Design of 1911.

Opposite: A very smart looking Stanier 2-6-4 tank No.42105 waits at Swanbourne, at the time the limit of operations on the Cambridge to Oxford line, ready to take over from Black 5 No.45292 on the LCGB "South Midlands" Rail tour of 17 October 1964. The tank headed the train via Bletchley to Wolverton to then traverse the freight-only Newport Pagnell Branch, before handing over again to the Black 5, which continued to Market Harborough where a 4F took over back to Bedford. Passenger traffic had ceased on the latter branch as recently as 7 September 1964. In recent times the through line to Oxford has been reinstated.

A pair of Stanier 2-6-4 tanks Nos.42574 and 42644 headed the "Conway Valley" rail tour on 24 September 1966 down the scenic country Conway Valley line to Blanenau Festiniog from Llandudno Junction. Here the tanks halt at the intermediate picturesque Bettsws-y-Coed Station for water and photographs.

The pair of Stanier 2-6-4 tanks Nos.42574 and 42644 enter Blanenau Festiniog with the LCGB "Conway Valley" rail tour under towering mountains of slate. After electric haulage to Crewe from Euston "Britannia" Pacific No.70004 "William Shakespeare" had hauled the train along the North Wales coast line to Llandudno Junction.

Later in the day the "Britannia" having rejoined the train at Llandudno Junction. had run back to Rhyl, where the last operational "Crab" 2-6-0 No.42942 took over. Here it pauses at Rhuddlan on the way down the by then freight-only branch to Denbigh from the junction at Rhyl, which once connected through to Corwen on the line from Ruabon to Barmouth. Only one more special with this "Crab", also noticeable by its damaged cylinder cover, occurred after this date. The "Britannia" then returned the train to Crewe followed by electric traction back to London. The passenger service between Rhyl and Denbigh was withdrawn on 19 September 1955 and Denbigh Shed – only recently modernized – lost all its allocation of engines.

"Royal Scot" Class No.46167 "The Hertfordshire Regiment" pulls out of
Birmingham New Street with a London-bound express on 6 February 1958.

A nicely clean Black 5 4-6-0 No.45299 departs into the subterranean gloom of the tunnels at the east end of Birmingham New Street with a train to Derby and beyond. (6.2.58)

Opposite: "Jubilee" Class No.45644 "Howe" starts the northbound "Pines Express" out of the dark depths at the east end of Birmingham New Street Station looking in gleaming condition. (6.2.58)

Working the northbound "Devonian" from Bristol "Jubilee" No.45685 "Barfleur" climbs the 1 in 37 of the Lickey Incline flat out on the wet rails even with a Pannier tank and Standard 9F No.92079 banking at the rear on a grey February day. (1.2.58)

Opposite: An interesting trio, consisting of a Fowler Class 4P 2-6-4 tank (No.42338) sandwiched between two ex Midland 3F 0-6-0s (the nearer one being No.43521), shunting outside Bournville Shed on 20 February 1957 in the winter sunshine.

Unfortunately the famous "Lickey Banker" ex MR 0-10-0 No.58100 had been withdrawn the previous year in May 1956. Standard 9F No.92079 was its replacement at this time and at least sported the old banker's headlight. It is here seen backing down the bank to Bromsgrove after banking a train. (2.2.57)

A southbound freight headed by 8F No.48700 eases gingerly onto the top of the 1 in 37 Lickey Incline out of Blackwell Station in the winter sunshine. (2.2.57)

NORTH WEST SCOTLAND

Post Grouping development of the McIntosh G.R. 439 Class 0-4-4T No.55263 climbs briskly up the valley on the 1.42p.m. from Killin to Killin Junction with its single coach on 23 August 1961 – about halfway up the branch with a young enthusiast on the footplate! The branch was a steep climb at 1 in 50 for the 4 mile trip and the branch locomotives normally faced the gradient. There was no loop at the station, and gravity shunting was used instead of running round. Killin Junction had no road access and only served to connect with main line trains on the Oban line.

The Killin Railway actually terminated at Loch Tay Station, but the latter was closed in1939. The branch engine continued to use the small running shed at Loch Tay for water and servicing. Here the Caledonian tank No.55263 is seen resting at the shed on the shores of Loch Tay between duties. The shed was a mile or so down from the station and the small station house here was used as a private dwelling at this time. After 1961 the branch engine used was usually a BR 2-6-4T until the closure of the Oban line south of Crianlarich in 1965, but seemed an overkill in power for such a duty.

BR Standard Class 5 No.73077 4-6-0 double heading with an LNER B1 (equipped with self-weighing tender) raise a smoke cloud as they attempt to start a heavy Fort William to Glasgow express out of Spean Bridge slipping in the pouring rain.

BR Class 5 No.73077 again makes a spirited departure from Fort William Station on the shores of Loch Linnhe with the 5.10p.m. to Glasgow on another dull wet day. In these days Fort William Station had quite an extensive layout with three platforms and was located right down on the quayside convenient for the loch steamers and transporting the fishing catches. (26.8.61)

K1 No.62034 threads typical rugged Mallaig extension scenery at the east end of Loch Eilt with a Mallaig-bound freight. 1961 was officially the last year for using steam on the West Highland line and the Mallaig extension. (26.8.61)

BR Class 5 No.73148 rounds the corner at the top of the climb of Glen Ogle on a train from Oban and the Caledonian route via Dunblane to Stirling and Glasgow Buchanan Street. (8.61)

North British Class J36 0-6-0 No. 65313 shunts the yard outside Fort William Shed. At this time several J36s were shedded at Fort William. (26.8.61)

8F No.48457 pounds up Shap from Tebay passing Scout Green box some 3 miles up the 5 mile climb at 1 in 75 to Shap summit with a heavy down freight, banked by a Fowler 2-6-4T No.42396 in the rear on 8 September 1960.

"Clan" Pacific No.72001 "Clan Cameron" steams down from Shap summit with the 9.43a.m. Liverpool Exchange – Edinburgh. (8.9.60)

Another LMS stalwart, albeit a smaller one this time on the Settle and Carlisle line. Horwich "Crab" 2-6-0 No.42905 masters the climb coming off the northern end of Ribblehead Viaduct heading for Carlisle with a line of flat wagons on a gradient of 1 in 100 for15 unrelenting miles from Settle Junction to Blea Moor Tunnel.

Opposite: Black 5 No.44905 pounds away up the northern ascent of Shap with a long southbound mixed freight at a somewhat lesser gradient of 1in 125, but lasting for11 miles, with only a 1 mile respite at Shap Station. (8.9.60)

"Britannia" Pacific No 70018 "Flying Dutchman" pulls out of Hawick Station with the down "Waverley Express"
over the Waverley route to Edinburgh with a woman holding her small boy waving good bye. (7.5.62)

LNER SPECIALS

LNER Class J11 0-6-0 No.64354 of original 1901 GC vintage leaves Eggington Junction after a photostop with the second leg of the LCGB "Midland Ltd" rail tour on 14 October 1962. It was en route from Nottingham Victoria to Burton on Trent via Derby Friargate where a Midland 3F 0-6-0 would take over. This tour was to be a last swansong for the class with this engine being one of the last 12 surviving by this date.

LNER A1 Class Pacific No.60128 "Bongrace" pulls away from Peterborough East on the second leg of the LCGB "Pennine Limited" rail tour which it headed as far as Sheffield (Victoria) via Retford and the electrified Penistone line, on the 19 September 1964, having taken over from a "Royal Scot". The train then continued behind a 2600 electric locomotive to Guide Bridge where a Stanier 2-6-0 took over back to Nottingham Victoria where the "Royal Scot" returned the special down the Great Central main line to Marylebone. (3.9.66)

B1 4-6-0 No.61360 takes the north curve of the triangle at Ambergate West Junction with the returning RCTS "High Peak" rail tour run on 27 June 1964. The engine had hauled the special to Parsley Hay from Sheffield Victoria via the Woodhead route (with electric locomotive assistance) to gain access to the western end of the Cromford and High Peak Railway, where the passengers continued in a train of guards vans to explore the C&HP line hauled by two J94 0-6-0 Saddle tanks. The B1 then picked up the passengers again at High Peak Junction for the return to Sheffield.

"Flying Scotsman" No.4472 in preserved LNER apple green livery, now in its original appearance with single chimney and no smoke deflectors at the coal tower at Cricklewood Shed on its second outing in preservation form after being bought by Alan Pegler for £3,000. It will haul the RPS "Great Central Special" of 15 June 1963 from Sheffield to London, and will return using the Great Central route.

Opposite: At Edinburgh Waverley on 25 June 1966, NB J37 0-6-0s Nos.64570 and 64618 prepare to leave with the second day of the Warwickshire Railway Society "Aberdonian" rail tour. They hauled the train to Anstruther, then the limit of the coast line to St Andrews, where the two engines were turned on the old turntable. This tour was the last run from London to Aberdeen and back with steam used all the way by using a circuitous route.

Preserved A3 "Flying Scotsman" waits to leave York with the WRS "Aberdonian" special of 25 June 1966 returning to London.

The privately restored K4 Class 2-6-0 "The Great Marquess" resplendent in apple green livery prepares to leave Keighley on the main line with the returning "Mercian" rail tour on 22 April 1967, the passengers having visited the Keighley and Worth Valley Railway.

Built between 1888 and 1900 by the North British Railway, one hundred and twenty eight J36s survived into BR ownership and a few even remained in service to the end of Scottish Steam in 1966. Here one of the last active members of the class, No.65345 takes water at Musselburgh, the terminus of a short branch off the East Coast main line, having run round Edinburgh starting at the Corstopine Branch with the Railway Society of Scotland's "J36" rail tour of 31 August 1966. The tour also visited Smeaton on the truncated remains of the branch that once led to Lauder. This date marked the end of steam in Scotland apart from one or two J36s retained at Bathgate Shed for colliery workings.

B16/2 Class 4-6-0 No.61438 pauses at Loughborough Central for photographs with the LCGB "Midland Ltd" tour on 14 October 1962, which it hauled from Marylebone to Nottingham Victoria where a GE J11 Class 0-6-0 took over to Burton-on-Trent. A B16 was a rare visitor to the south of the country, but unfortunately the light was misty and poor at Loughborough.

One of the last operational B1s No.61131 of Wakefield Shed, having taken water and used the turntable, runs round at Nottingham Victoria to head the last day LCGB "Great Central Farwell" rail tour as far as Elsecar Junction and the electrified Penistone line, double heading with sister engine B1 No.1173 on 3 September 1966. The train had rather bizarrely been headed to Nottigham Victoria by "Merchant Navy" Pacific No.35030 "Elder Dempster Lines" starting from Waterloo. On the following day the Great Central line between Calvert and Rugby was closed.

CONSETT ORE LINE

Another joy of exploring the North East was the Consett ore line. There 600 ton loads of iron ore from the coast at Tyne Dock were hauled up the steep gradient nearly all the way from South Pelaw Junction to the steelworks at Consett by 9Fs banked by a second 9F at the other end. The sight of two 9Fs, working flat out at each end of the train will be remembered for a long time. The gradient up to the summit at Anfield Plain was continuous at 1 in 50 to 1 in 40 for 2 miles on the total climb of 10 miles. The 9Fs had relatively recently taken over from the Q7s on this duty as can be seen by the air pumps still fitted to both classes, which were required to open the wagons' hopper doors and discharge their loads at the steelworks.

2-10-0 9F No.92097 comes down the line from Consett with an empty ore train to South Pelaw Junction near Pelton, while Q6 No.63394 shunts its coal wagons on the NCB lines. (1.8.61)

Opposite: 9F 2-10-0 No.92066 reaches the summit of the climb to Anfield Plain en route to Consett with a 600-ton load of iron ore. The banker has just dropped off at the rear (May 1962).

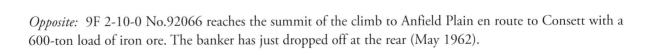

2-10-0 No.92065 makes an impressive sight as it crosses the tracks at South Pelaw with a loaded ore train and is about to take a banker (another 9F) to head up the grades to Consett. A Q6 and other 9F bankers can be seen awaiting the next duty in the distance past the signal box. (1.9.62)

J39 0-6-0 No.64713 keeps to the near line as it passes the signal box at Pelaw with a haul of empty coal wagons for the collieries. (1.9.61)

9F No.92066 rounds the curve past Greencroft Cottages to the summit at Anfield Plain working hard with double chimney 9F No. 92167 blasting along at the back with the 600-ton load. (8.5.62)

Q6 0-8-0 No.63365 makes much ado of hauling a light coal train up to the summit of the line to Consett east of Anfield Plain past Greenfield Cottages. (1.9.61)

Looking freshly ex-works Q7 No.63465 heads up the Consett ore line to pick up a coal train from a local colliery. This was the only Q7 I ever saw even reasonably clean, while again two 9Fs and a Q6 are waiting in the distance. (1.9.61)

This side-on picture shows a complete ore train between Beamish and Stanley with a
9F at each end and the nine ore wagons carrying its 600-ton load of iron ore. (8.5.62)

Q7 No. 63460 starts the climb to Consett with a train of flat wagons.(1.9.61). This engine was subsequently preserved and ran on several specials in BR livery, one of which is shown in a following section before being taken over by the NELPG and is now based at the NYMR.

Close up of banker 9F No.92167, one of the three 9Fs fitted experimentally with a mechanical stoker and believed to be under test on the line at this time, waiting at the junction for its next banking duty, while a Q6 runs past en route to Tyne Dock. (8.5.62)

Semi-silhouette shot of 9F No.92097 working away up the heavy grade past Stanley with a Tyne Dock – Consett ore train. (7.5.63)

1965 SCOTTISH RAMBLER

Built by Sharp Stewart & Co in 1894, Highland Railway "Jones Goods" 4-6-0 No.103, another pre-Grouping locomotive restored by the Scottish Region, has a particular place in Britain's railway history – it was the first 4-6-0 to operate on a British railway. Withdrawn by the LMS in 1934, it was like No.123 preserved by the company. It was restored to operational condition in 1959 and ran a number of specials including on the "Scottish Rambler" tours. The "Jones Goods" is pictured here leaving Paisley St James with the 1965 "Scottish Rambler" on 17 April 1965 (having previously traversed the branch from East Kilbride and Linwood and other goods branches around Glasgow) and heads for Greenock Princes Pier via the Caledonian route.

A4 Pacific, No.60031 "Golden Plover" pauses for water at Galashiels en route from Edinburgh over the "Waverley" route to Carlisle with the 1965 "Scottish Rambler" on 18 April 1965. Unfortunately on this day the weather deteriorated, but was later seen returning to Glasgow up Beattock Bank in the fading light and snow showers.

One of the most popular preserved locomotives of the quartet preserved by the Scottish Region was the Caledonian Railway "Single" No.123, preserved in Caledonian blue livery. With the two Caledonian coaches, it is pictured between Glasgow Central and Edinburgh Princes Street near Merchiston with the second part of the Easter SLS/BLS 1965 "Scottish Rambler" on 19 April 1965. The first part was headed by "Gordon Highlander" to Edinburgh Waverley from Glasgow. On their individual arrivals in the middle of the day BR Class 3 78000 Class 2-6-0s had headed the two portions separately between Leith Central and Edinburgh Princes Street and Edinburgh Waverley Stations, and vice versa, to connect up with the two preserved engines ready to return to Carstairs – a somewhat complicated scenario!

Preserved GNSR No.49 (ex BR D40 Class ex No.62277) pauses at Midcalder en route from Glasgow Central to Edinburgh Waverley and Leith Central, where a BR 78000 Class 2-6-0 took over via Balerno Junction and then to Edinburgh Princes Street with the first part of the 1965 "Scottish Rambler" joint rail tour of the Stephenson Locomotive Society and the Branch Line Society. The other part of the train was hauled by the Caledonian Single 4-2-2 No.123 with two Caledonian coaches to Edinburgh Princes Street. This was thought to be the last time either engine appeared in use on a special before being incarcerated in the museum at Glasgow. Ex Great North of Scotland Railway 4-4-0 No.49 "Gordon Highlander" was restored to its pre-Grouping livery by the Scottish Region. Designed by Pickersgill, the 21 locomotives of the class were built between 1898 and 1920, the last eight, of which No.49 was one, were built with superheaters and extended smokeboxes. The class was progressively withdrawn between 1947 and 1958, "Gordon Highlander" being the last to be withdrawn and then preserved.

GNSR 4-4-0 No.49 "Gordon Highlander" (ex BR Class D40 No.62277) backs down onto Edinburgh St Margaret's Shed having headed the first part of the SLS/BLS 1965 "Scottish Rambler" from Glasgow via Edinburgh Waverley to Leith Central on 19 April 1965. Later in the day the "Soldier" headed its train to Carstairs via Midcalder Junction and Auchengray, while CR "Single" 123 headed the first part of the train from Edinburgh Princes Street.

The "Jones Goods" at Glasgow General Terminus Goods Depot while working the second day of the 1965 "Scottish Rambler".
The first day involved a 2-6-0 "Crab" on a brake van train, but the weather was appalling and virtually un-photographable. (17.4.65)

The preserved Highland Railway 4-6-0 No.103 pounds up the gradient of 3½ miles at 1 in 70 followed by 2 miles at 1 in 98 up to Port Glasgow Summit out of Greenock Princes Pier in the fading light of an April evening in 1965, with the Clyde and the Dumbartonshire Hills visible in the distance. No.103 was returning along the former GSWR line via Bridge of Weir to Glasgow with the SLS/BLS "Scottish Rambler" on 17 April 1965.

Opposite: One of the last times it was worked in preservation the preserved "Jones Goods" No.103 climbs upgrade near Hairmyres en route to East Kilbride via Busby Junction from Glasgow St Enoch before returning to Glasgow General Terminus Goods Depot on the second day of the 1965 "Scottish Rambler".

A4 Pacific No.60031 "Golden Plover" speeds up the 10 miles at a gradient of 1 in 70 up to Falahill Summit near Tynehead with the southbound "Scottish Rambler" from Edinburgh to Carlisle over the Waverley route on 18 April 1965.

The C.R. "Single" and caledonian coaches pulls smartly away from Auchengray after taking water and a photostop on route to Carstairs with the first part of the "Scottish Rambler" on the fourth and final day.

Following on from the CR Single "Gordon Highlander" makes smoke as it approaches Auchengray for a photostop heading the second part of the 1965 "Scottish Rambler" on 19 April 1965 en route from Edinburgh to Carstairs.

Having run as separate parts of the four-day 1965 "Scottish Rambler" tour the "Caledonian Single" and "Gordon Highlander" join up at Carstairs to haul the re-joined train back to Glasgow double headed at the end of the tour. This was the last time I believe these two lovely engines were seen in operation.

NORTH EASTERN SPECIALS
SCARBOROUGH • WHITBY • NEWCASTLE

Well turned out ex LNER B1 Class 4-6-0 No.61031 "Reedbuck" en route up the hilly coast line to Whitby with the RCTS "North Eastern Limited" tour held on 2 May 1964 pounds up the steep gradient and round the equally steep curve into Staintondale Station on the climb from Scarborough to Ravenscar. A mile or so further on the B1 came to a stand on the wet rails while trying to make the sharp climb to Ravenscar summit. The B1 had come on the special at York after the arrival of the train from Newcastle behind an A3 pacific; the train had then travelled via Malton to Scarborough behind the B1. It may be noted that all intermediate stations between York and Scarborough except Malton and Seamer were closed to all traffic on 22 September 1930.

Later the last operational ex NE Q7 0-8-0 No.63460, already a preserved engine, departs from Middlesborough Station making an energetic exhaust en route to Newcastle via Wellfield and Sunderland with the last leg of the RCTS "Great Eastern Ltd" rail tour in the fading light. The 15 engines in this class were the most powerful 0-8-0s in Britain. Nos.901 to 905 had a tractive effort of 36,963 lbs. When new they were to be found at various N.E. sheds, but were gradually all concentrated at Tyne Dock, where they did yeomen service on the Consett ore trains. On trial on the Scottish Region in 1923 903 made several trips up the bank between Bridge of Earn and Glenfarg, and on the last trip she lifted around 780 tons without difficulty. They were all withdrawn en bloc at the end of 1962, except for 63460 which was preserved in working order and became one of the NEPLG engines for use on the North Yorkshire Moors Railway. (2.5.64)

The RCTS "North Eastern Ltd" tour was held in unfortunately poor weather, and the B1 No.61031 slipped to a stand with the wet rails while attempting the very sharp climb from Flying Hall up to the Ravenscar summit on the coastline from Scarborough to Whitby. "Reedbuck" had to set back several times, with much sanding of the rails by the fireman, before the gradient was finally surmounted.

On arrival at Whitby, which involved reversing down from the high level station of Whitby West Cliff (the coast line being already closed beyond this point), the B1 shunted the sidings outside the station, with the ruined Whitby Abbey on the skyline across the river, in readiness to continue to Middlesborough via Battersby Junction, where the last ex NE Q7 0-8-0 No.64360 took over for the final leg to Newcastle. (2.5.64)

The last active K1 No.62005 stops at Leyburn Station with its diesel help, returning from Redmire to the main line at Northallerton and then to the Richmond Branch via Eyholme Junction. The station is a centre of operation for the Wensleydale Railway preserved line, which now operates to Leeming Bar and Northallerton West from Redmire. Forty years later a repeat "Three Dales" train with the same K1 travelled the line with diesel assistance at the rear and a better-looking train of maroon coaches. This K1 is now preserved and is based on the NYMR, as well as hauling specials on the public railway network.

Opposite: One of the last active K1 Class 2-6-0s in immaculate condition from Heaton Shed, Newcastle, pilots a Class 25 diesel away from Redmire, the limit of the truncated Wensleydale Branch from Northallerton, which formerly ran the 39 miles through to Hawes and Garsdale, on 20 May 1967. The SLS "Three Dales" tour was the last steam-hauled enthusiast special in this area of the North East and the last steam train to traverse this branch until recent times. Bolton Castle can be seen on the skyline behind the train. The engine was thankfully preserved and restored to working order by the NELPG. The branch had fortunately been kept open to this point for freight only to serve the limestone works seen at the back of the train, but the passenger service to Hawes had been withdrawn on 26 April 1954. Further limestone quarries could previously also be found at Wensley and other places on the line, serving the Teesside furnaces. Parcels trains continued to work between Northallerton and Leyburn after the withdrawal of passenger services, and goods traffic continued to work through to Hawes. Freight traffic continued until 27 April 1964, when the section west of Redmire was closed completely.

Here the K1, now without diesel assistance, having reversed direction heads up the Military Branch to Catterick Camp with the SLS "Three Dales" rail tour from Catterick Bridge the junction on the Richmond Branch. The branch had some steep sections including a 1½ mile climb at 1 in 50 after the bridge over the River Swale. The branch had several unmanned level crossings which had to be manned by railway or military personnel. The final passenger working over the branch to Catterick Camp was made by a diesel multiple unit railcar on 26 October 1964.

After running round at Catterick Camp the "Three Dales" tour then continued up the 10 mile branch to Richmond. Here the K1 prepares to leave the attractive terminus at Richmond before heading for the Weardale Branch. Richmond Branch passenger trains were withdrawn in March 1969. Freight traffic to Catterick Bridge continued until 9 February 1970, and later that year work commenced on dismantling the Camp line and the Richmond Branch itself.

Having reached the Weardale Branch via Darlington and Bishop Aukland, the K1 62005 steams round a sharp curve between Wolsingham and Stanhope on the run up the line to Westgate-in-Weardale with the last stage of the SLS "Three Dales" tour, just after a rain storm and a change in the weather for the worse. Passenger trains to Wearhead were withdrawn on 29 June 1953 but the line was kept open to serve the cement works at Eastgate. The Weardale Branch had in the past been intensively used for the extraction of various minerals. Fortunately part of this attractive branch is now being operated as the preserved Weardale Railway, at present only over the section from Stanhope to Wolsingham.

NORTH EAST – ASHINGTON

One of the last of five operational "Jubilees" retained at Leeds Holbeck Shed, for operation over the Leeds – Carlisle line, No.45562 "Alberta" slows for signals at Winning North Junction having just crossed the viaduct over the Wansbeck River, after leaving Ashington in Northumberland with the returning SLS/Manchester Locomotive Society – "Ashington" rail tour on 11 June 1967. At Ashington an extensive tour of the colliery system was made by a National Coal Board 0-6-2 T seen on the next page. This was nearly the last steam special in the North East and "Alberta" was destined to be one of the last of the class to be withdrawn in September 1967, but unfortunately was not preserved unlike No.45593 "Kolhaphur".

The "Jubilee" had headed the tour from Manchester Exchange to the extensive colliery railway at Ashington. So large was the Ashington Coal Company's system, built to serve the various collieries, that it operated a twenty-four hour passenger service, comprising some 94 passenger trains a day from Monday to Friday for the miners, but this service had been transferred to buses in 1966. Here NCB 0-6-0T No.39 (built by Robert Stephenson and Hawthorn in 1954 and scrapped in 1969) is seen with such a train traversing the circuit with the tour passengers housed in old suburban coaches, the first two being North Eastern Railway eliptical-roof non-corridors and the third a Furness Railway non-corridor coach. The large Lynemouth Colliery on the system was the last working pit in the North East and finished production in January 2005, due to flooding of the subsea coal workings which ran many miles out from the coast.

LMS & LNER SHEDS

Line up at Woodford Halse Shed: from left to right Black 5 44732, 8F 48002, 8F 48395, Black 5 45299, a 2-6-4T and another Class 5 on 7 March 1965. It is hard to believe that all this would be gone only a few months later with the shed closing on 14 June 1965.

An immaculate "Jubilee" 4-6-0 No.45708 "Resolution" gleams in the sunshine outside the relatively small Monument Lane Shed, the only LMS Shed in central Birmingham itself. The "Jubilee" has the earlier Fowler tender with the coal containing rails. (3.3.1957)

"Royal Scots" lined up outside Annersley shed in the winter sunshine on 28 November 1964 – already stripped of their number and name plates and presumably on the point of withdrawal? Annersley Shed closed in January 1966 with the demise in Great Central traffic and the following complete closure of a large part of the line on 3 September 1966.

B1 4-6-0 No.61407 and WD 2-8-0 No.90441 are prominent in Thornton Junction Shed yard in company with other WDs and B1s, as well as diesels. Not long before the end of steam in Scotland at the end of August 1966.

On 17 May 1964 this date still finds an immaculate "Duchess" inside Rugby Shed, still appropriately wearing the Willesden Shed code, No.46245 "City of London". This is a very late date to find a "Duchess" in the South Midlands/London area. This could have been retained here in readiness to head a last special behind a "Duchess" to London with an Ian Allan tour on 1 September 1964 ending at London Paddington.

The inside of one of York Shed's roundhouses finds a gleaming V2 2-6-2 No.60961 and an immaculate B1 4-6-0 No. 61031 "Reedbuck" prepared in readiness for taking over the RCTS "North Eastern Limited" rail tour on 1 May 1964.

During a visit to Crewe Works on a bleak February day with snow on the ground an immaculate "Duchess" No.46227 "Duchess of Devonshire" and un-rebuilt "Patriot" No. 45543 "Home Guard" were to be seen outside the paint shop at Crewe. "Home Guard" was destined to be one of the last un-rebuilt "Patriots" left in service.

9F No.92096 and 8F 48057 on shed at Annersley on a fine winter's day. Note the amount of ash and debris around the shed roads, an indication of one reason for many to wish to switch over to relatively clean diesel. (28.11.64)

"Jinty" 0-6-0T No.47611 on duty at Cricklewood Shed, already with diesels present. (5.6.63)

An unusually clean 8F No.48057 on shed at Annersley being serviced on 28 November 1964.

One of the original ROD 04/1 2-8-0s No.43707 of Robinson GC 1911 vintage in steam in the yards at Colwick Shed. This date of 28 November 1964 was relatively late for such an old lady.

LAST MONTHS OF STEAM
IN THE NORTH WEST

The crew mounts up into the last surviving "Britannia" Pacific No.70013 "Oliver Cromwell" (beautifully turned out and still with nameplates) about to leave Fleetwood with the RCTS "Lancastrian No.2" tour, the train having arrived from Liverpool behind immaculate Black 5 No.45156 "Ayrshire Yeomanry" on 20 April 1968. The "Britannia" then hauled the train via Preston to Windermere via the LMS main line, and returned after turning to Morecambe Promenade where "Black Fives" took over again. By this time the the "Britannia" was already a special engine being kept at Carnforth. She is now preserved in working order and out running on specials around the rail network.

The last active Britannia No.70013 "Oliver Cromwell" speeds away from Preston towards Hogton en route from Manchester and Preston to Carnforth via Blackburn and Hellifield with the first leg of the Severn Valley Railway Society/Manchester Railway Touring Society "Steam Farewell" tour of 28 July 1968 with the willow herb in full bloom. The train had been diesel-hauled from Birmingham to Stockport where 70013 had taken over.

By now one of the most well used of the preserved Black 5s and seen regularly on the main line Black 5 No.45305 speeds through the closed station of Lymm near Warrington on the ex LNWR route from Liverpool to Manchester London Road via Speke and Widnes with the LCGB "Lancastrian" rail tour of 6 April 1968, which it headed throughout. The Black 5 returned from Manchester using the L&Y line to Southport and then via the coast line to Liverpool Docks.

Black 5s 45073 and 45156 storm through Cherry Tree with the MRTS/SVRS "Farewell to Steam" special on 27 July 1968 en route from Skipton to Bolton and Blackburn via a circuitous route that would tale in Lostock Hall Junction and Chorley.

After arrival of "Britannia" No.70013 from Fleetwood, an immaculate Black 5 No.45156 "Ayshire Yeomanry" with the fun fair in the background prepares to leave Morecambe Promenade with the RCTS "Lancastrian No.2" tour on 20 April 1968. It would double head with another Black 5 (No.45342) to Heysham Harbour before returning to Morecambe once more and proceeding back to Preston via Hellifield and Blackburn, where the pair would hand over again to 70013 for the return to Liverpool.

Having worked from Manchester Victoria via Stalybridge and Copy Pit, Black 5s Nos.44871 and 44894 storm up the southern ascent to Sough Tunnel near Spring Vale from Blackburn returning to Liverpool and Stockport via Bolton with the first of the SLS "Farewell to Steam" specials from Birmingham on 4 August 1968, one week before the official farewell to steam. This was the day after the cessation of steam haulage in normal service on British Railways and my penultimate photograph of BR steam.

A rear view of Black 5s Nos. 44871 and 44894 climbing away towards Sough Tunnel on 4 August 1968 with the first SLS special.

A short time later in the other direction "Britannia" "Oliver Cromwell" pilots Black 5 No. 44781 down the grade from Sough Tunnel with the LCGB "Farewell to Steam" special to Blackburn, where the train would be taken over by 8F No.48773 piloting the Black 5.